BRITAIN IN OLD PHOT

ACTON

THOMAS & AVERIL HARPER SMITH

ALAN SUTTON PUBLISHING LIMITED

Alan Sutton Publishing Limited
Phoenix Mill · Far Thrupp · Stroud
Gloucestershire · GL5 2BU

First published 1995

Front cover photograph: Crown Street, 1935.
Back cover photograph: T. Poore & Son, Park Royal, *c*. 1905.

British Library Cataloguing in Publication Data.
A catalogue record for this book is available from the British Library.

ISBN 0-7509-0943-9

Typeset in 9/10 Sabon.
Typesetting and origination by
Alan Sutton Publishing Limited.
Printed in Great Britain by
WBC Limited, Bridgend.

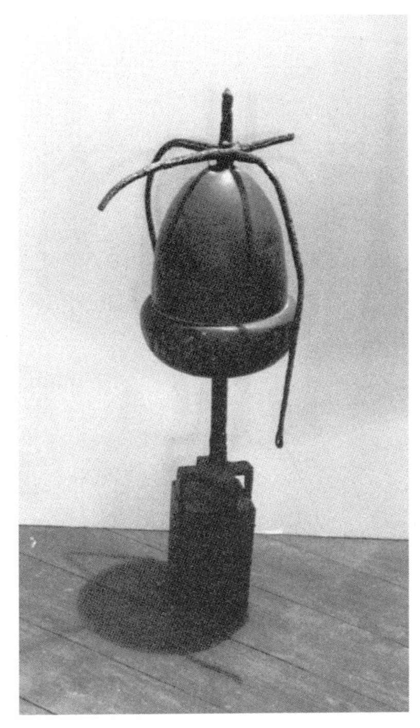

The acorn that stood on St Mary's parish church from 1588 to 1810 (it is now in the north aisle). Acton means 'oak settlement'.

Contents

The Entry into Acton: a watercolour of Acton as a rural parish, 1790. The girl on the left is going to the village well.

Introduction

This is not a history of Acton – it is not even a portrait. Rather it is a series of glimpses of a period of rapid change. It was not always so – for eight or nine hundred years from Saxon times, Acton hardly changed at all. In these early days there was one large estate on the west which in the Middle Ages was shared between St Paul's Cathedral and St Bartholomew's Priory, Smithfield, worked from two moated farms in the north. The relics of the moats, now gone, can be seen on pp. 64 and 66 and in the name Friar's Place. The village itself grew round St Mary's Church which the Bishop of London built in the twelfth century on the Uxbridge Road, for Acton was part of his manor of Fulham. Round it were the four great common fields, farmed in strips. A famous miniaturist, J.C.D. Engleheart, who retired to East Acton, made sketches of these in 1820 (see p. 8). The Uxbridge Road added to the prosperity of the village, for it ran from Tyburn (Marble Arch) some five miles to Acton, making the transport of crops easy, and further to the royal palace at Woodstock and later to the University of Oxford – thus there was much traffic which benefited the Acton inns that sprang up on the route.

At the Reformation the western estate passed into secular hands, but it made no difference to the farmers who leased the land. No wars troubled the village, except in 1642 when the Parliamentary force – which made its 'stand off' at Turnham Green while Prince Rupert covered the retreat of the Royalists from Brentford – vented its frustration in sacking Chiswick and Acton churches and pillaging the farmers' crops.

The biggest excitement was the discovery of minerals in three wells near Old Oak at the end of the seventeenth century. Acton Wells became a small spa with its assembly room and hotel (see p. 73). Several villas were built, and bottled water was sold in London. Next came the cutting of the Grand Junction Canal in 1801 in the north which facilitated the transport of hay to London. This was followed by the laying of the Great Western Railway through Acton in 1837, but there was no station at Acton until 1868. There was, however, an Acton station on the line later called the North London (later Acton Central) from 1853, at the beginning of the period of great change for the village.

In our first section, 'Early Days', we have tried to show a little of this earlier Acton, before the change occurred, and the few buildings that survived.

In 1859 the common fields were enclosed, and building began almost at once on the Turnham field and on the Church field. Many small houses were erected in the south, occupied by labourers from all over the country, and soon became overcrowded. Their wives took in washing and so initiated Acton's great laundry industry, stimulated by purpose-built premises. Six hundred laundry sites have been found (see p. 84).

The vast increase in population was accompanied by developments in local government, from Acton Local Board (1865) to District Council (1894) to Borough (1921). Transport to London increased, with trams to Shepherd's Bush for the railway (1873), buses and underground trains. Other estates were built further from the centre.

The brickfields on either side of the Vale, Acton's second main industry, were, at least on the south side, seen as factory sites: from 1901 a large number of industrial works were erected there, mainly in the engineering and the developing motor car sectors (see section three, p. 29). After the failure of the Agricultural Exhibition in the north of Acton, at Park Royal (the name given to it by the Royal Agricultural Society), this too became a major industrial area after the First World War (see pp. 70–2). It is said that between the wars Acton had more industry per square mile than Birmingham. After the Second World War, relocation and reorganization took these firms away. There was a major clearance of the little houses, particularly in the south, which were replaced by tower blocks and small industrial estates.

It is largely these changes that are shown in this book. We have tried to use as few familiar scenes as possible: many of our pictures have not been published before; indeed, many have not been seen outside our immediate circle. This will leave obvious gaps, which is in the nature of glimpses.

Section One

EARLY DAYS

The village pump, which stood on the edge of the narrow High Street from 1819, replacing the troughs fed from the Conduit field well maintained by a bequest of 1612 from Thomas Thorney. With the coming of mains water it went out of use in 1873.

The Church field, one of the four great common fields, sketched by J.C.D. Engleheart, 1820. The view is looking west towards the church and the wall of Acton House.

The eastern end of the same field, also sketched by Engleheart in 1820, with the windmill that stood there from *c.* 1800 to 1860.

St Mary's parish church in 1790. This colourwash by an unknown artist shows the medieval chancel, the bricked-up nave and the Tudor tower with cupola and acorn (see p. 2).

The village stocks. The date and artist of this pencil sketch are unknown. The stocks were in the High Street by The Mount (see p. 22) and the church entrance, but were removed before 1880.

The walls of Acton. A schoolboy in 1866 wrote 'Acton is a queer sort of place, very old, with great high walls all round.' Above left are the walls of Berrymead Priory (see p. 26); on the right are the walls of Suffolk and Lichfield Houses, built in 1737. Below right are the walls of Woodlands, the home of the Briggs family from the eighteenth century. On the left, tram No. 17 passes the council offices *en route* to Shepherd's Bush, shortly after the section between Shepherd's Bush and Acton Depot opened for electric traction on 4 April 1901.

The wall round Hill House, Acton Hill, which was Springfield College (a private commercial school for boys) from 1890 to 1909.

The Elms, the last of the eighteenth-century villas. It was built in 1725 on the site of a mill; Samuel Wegg added the wings on either side in 1750; in 1889 it became an electricity works and it is now Twyford Church of England High School.

The parish church in 1837. By then it was bricked up and the cupola and acorn had been taken down.

West Lodge in Uxbridge Road, which was built in 1800 by John Winter of Heathfield Lodge (see p. 98) after a design by John Soane. The photograph was taken during an Acton History Society visit, June 1964.

The first parish infant school, in Oldham Terrace, 1837 (see p. 49). From 1926 to 1976 it was Acton Special School; it is now used by St Mary's Church as a parish hall.

'Bellevue', a terrace of five houses, shown here in 1838. They still stand in the High Street.

Orchard Place, East Acton. This was built in around 1860 and is still standing.

The first Wesleyan church and school, Gunnersbury Lane, 1857. The buildings still exist.

Section Two

DOWN THE HIGH STREET

The milepost from the Turnpike Road outside St Mary's Church, which dates from 1832. The High Road was turnpiked from 1714.

The tram depot at the west end of the High Street, which opened in 1896 for the London United Tramways. It is now the bus depot.

A tramways wheel carrier, *c.* 1933, with a bus and a type T tram behind. The Elms Parade shopping centre (built 1931) is in the background.

A horse tram, decorated for Queen Victoria's Diamond Jubilee in 1897, standing outside the depot.

The old Red Lion Inn in 1895. It dated from 1740 but was demolished and rebuilt in 1906, when it was joined with the Pineapple pub.

The laying of the foundation stone of the new Acton Hill Wesleyan church, 1906.

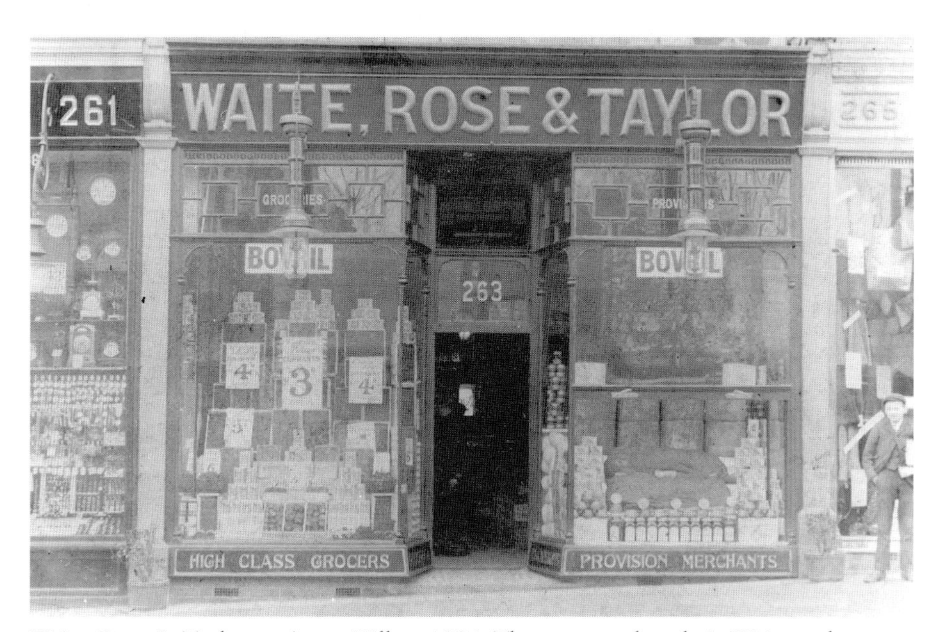

Waite, Rose & Taylor on Acton Hill, *c.* 1906. The supermarket chain Waitrose began at 263 High Street, and spread outwards from Acton and Chiswick.

No. 237 High Street. Henry Mitchell, parish clerk for forty years, carpenter, sexton, undertaker and Acton historian, was born here; he died in 1914. Next door is Morgan's the watchmaker's, with their huge clock.

Nos 201–7 High Street in 1890. The entry on the right is to the Cock and Crown Yard, the site of an ancient inn. On the left is the Six Bells.

Looking east along the High Street in 1890. On the left is Virginia House, dated 1740 and the third of three eighteenth-century houses, then come more shops and the Old King's Head. The 'Old King' is Charles I.

Mr A.T. Overall (on the right) with 'the largest horse collar in the world', 1895. Overall's the leather merchant's stood at No. 238 High Street, to the left of the picture above.

Looking west down the High Street to the Old King's Head, *c.* 1885. On the right is The Mount, on the left Baker's Stores.

The Old King's Head, *c.* 1890. It was named in 1664 after Charles I, but was probably much older still.

The Mount, *c.* 1890 (demolished 1893). It was so called because of steps up from the road. On this small triangle were twelve shops, with others behind.

Fire at the King's Head in 1926. It had been set back and rebuilt in 1894, with a storey added in 1921.

Looking east along the High Street from the church in 1906. There is a bank (established 1887; now Barclays) on the left, with a bus outside. Warren & Beck's the draper's (established 1889) is on the right.

The George and Dragon in 1893. It was a well-known coaching inn, having been on this site from 1737. By 1873 it had become a small pub.

The Wellington (Acton Brewery Tap), which opened in 1870. Acton Brewery was in Church Road from 1866 to 1908.

The Wellington, ready for demolition in 1911.

Nos 156–64 High Street (Beauchamp's Market), in 1910. It opened in 1888 as the first superstore. On the left is Mitchell's Penny Bazaar which by 1924 was Marks & Spencer's.

Looking west from Beauchamp's before 1901. On the left is the new Parade, partially built. The Wellington is still there. One solitary horse-tram wends its way along the road.

The interior of Our Lady of Lourdes Roman Catholic Church in 1906. The church was opened in 1902 and the sanctuary decorations were completed in 1904.

Berrymead Priory in 1905. Built by Sir John Trevor in 1666, it was gothicized and called a priory by Thomas Clutton in 1802. It was never a religious house, and was demolished in 1980.

Grove House, *c.* 1900, when it was a commercial school. It was built around 1800. Acton Council bought the site in 1924 and sold some of the land for shops.

Acton Technical College, *c.* 1934. It was built in 1928 for Middlesex County Council.

Applied Mechanics Lab at Acton Technical College, *c.* 1934. Trade courses were advertised at 10*s* to 15*s* per session.

No. 1 High Street, the Railway Tavern, *c.* 1905. First built in 1873, it was rebuilt by Alfred Savigear in 1898–9 to the design of Edward Monson.

Section Three

ALONG THE VALE

Brick made at East Acton brickworks in the Vale, c. *1880. By 1900 the brickfields either side of the Vale were giving way to factories.*

View over the factory area from the roof of C.A. Vandervell's & Co. (CAV) in the 1920s. Clearly visible are Eastman's, Napier's and the 1913 CAV building in Warple Way.

Queen Mary visiting the Eastman's factory in February 1927. Eastman's, the dyers and cleaners, came to the Vale in 1900.

St Barnabas Mission Church, *c.* 1960. It was established in 1892 to serve the poorest district of Acton, but was taken over by Eastman's in 1919 as their social club.

Making aero engines at D. Napier & Sons in the 1920s. D. Napier & Sons were in Acton from 1903 to 1963; their engines gained many speed records.

A newspaper photograph of the Napier-engined Supermarine flying boat which won the Schneider Trophy in 1927. Napier engines also powered the Bluebird which took Sir Malcolm Campbell to the land-speed record in 1927, and the aeroplane that captured the air-speed record in 1928.

Fire in 1914 at C.A. Vandervell's & Co., electricians and motor ignition specialists. In Warple Way from 1909, CAV were the largest employer of labour in Acton.

CAV–Bosch works outing, September 1933. The factory closed for the day and 'Bluebell' motor coaches took 650 workers and staff to Margate. A band accompanied the procession.

W. & G. Cabs lined up in Larden Road in 1910. They featured the four-cylinder 15 h.p. Napier engine and were part of the 1,000 cab fleet of W. & G. Du Cros of Acton, renowned for its smart livery and uniformed drivers.

Stewart & Ardern's, *c.* 1949. Outside is a pre-1952 model of the Morris Oxford Series MO saloon. The showroom and extensive service area for Morris cars was opened in 1926.

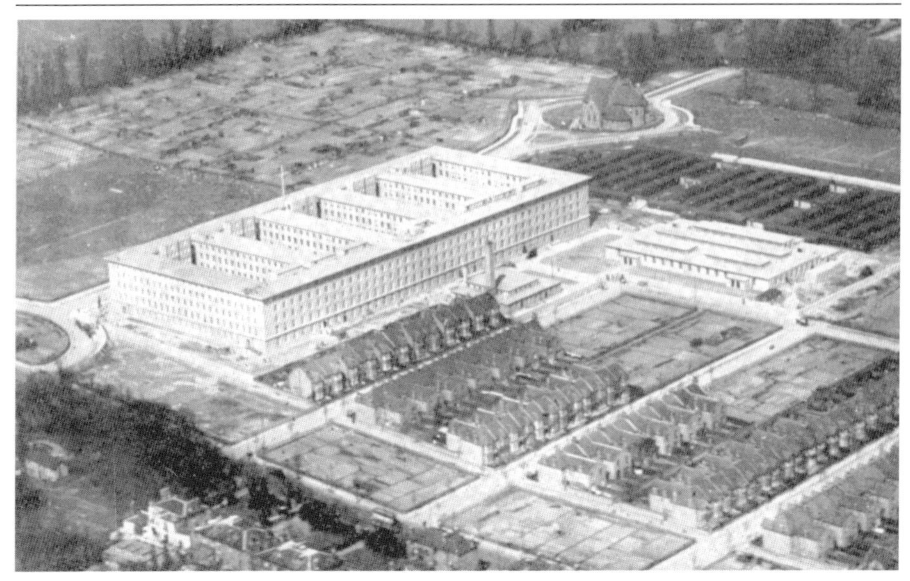

Aerial view north of the Vale. Prominent are the government buildings, opened in 1921 to deal with war pensions and employing 3,000 clerks. Houses of the First, Second and Third avenues are on the right, St Thomas's Church to the north.

Church of St Thomas the Apostle, Bromyard Avenue, which was consecrated in 1915 and replaced St Barnabas (see p. 32). It was intended as the focus of the new Goldsmith's Livery Company estate (see p. 110).

The chancel arch of St Thomas, showing the rood beam that was the church's war memorial. In 1980 the church was sold to the Ethiopian Church. It was vacant by 1990.

Demolition of the church after the fire of November 1992. Flats are now on the site.

The King's Arms, which moved to the corner of East Acton Lane in 1885. The wide forecourt was to be a stopping place for the trams of the London General Omnibus Co. (see p. 45).

The Salvation Army band playing in Acton Park in 1922.

Section Four

OFF THE HIGH STREET

Market Place, formerly part of Horn Lane, 1960. A trolley bus passes the east end of the church and the William IV pub at the junction with Horn Lane.

The junction of Market Place and Churchfield Road in 1970.

Trams standing at the end of Horn Lane for Edgware routes, *c.* 1936. Wires for the new trolley buses can be seen, and one of the first 'Belisha' crossings.

Horn Lane looking south in 1917. On the left is Hiron the blacksmith's. In the distance you can make out the castellated Blue Anchor, on the left Springfield House.

Gould's forge near the corner of Stuart Road in 1908. The poster advertises the horse show to take place on the Green, East Acton, on Whit Monday.

Digging up Horn Lane to lay tram tracks in 1909. On the extreme left is the Old Rectory, on the right the Duke of York.

The Duke of York at the entrance to the Steyne, *c.* 1905.

Wales Farm Dairy of J. Franks, 182 Horn Lane, *c.* 1910.

Baldwin's Empire Laundry in the Steyne, *c.* 1913. It was there from 1898 to 1917 and was said to be London's largest laundry (see also p. 104).

Aerial view of the Steyne, *c.* 1960. The CWS jam factory has replaced the laundry, and on the left is the Acorn Telephone Exchange, opened in 1932.

Old cottages and the Blue Anchor in the Steyne, 1895. They were later called East Row, and were demolished in 1935 to make way for council flats.

Cottages and the Jubilee Almshouses in 1967. The almshouses were built in 1888 to commemorate the Golden Jubilee of Queen Victoria; they were demolished with the cottages in 1972 for road improvements.

The London General Omnibus garage in Lexden Road, the Steyne, 1964. It was built in 1892 and included accommodation for the horses.

King Street (formerly Back Lane) in 1895. The wall of St Mary's Church is on the left; on the right is the 'postmen's office' of 1895.

King Street from the High Street, 1906.

St Mary's parish church interior, *c.* 1900. Note the north gallery, which was taken down in 1950.

Mill Hill Terrace, *c.* 1905.

Crown Street, south of the High Street, in 1935. In 1903 the council acquired Woodlands, to enable the building of a secondary school and set up a park (see p. 102). It laid out a new road to link the High Street with the south in 1909. The land on either side was acquired by T. Poore & Son, who in the 1920s built shops and a covered market on the right-hand side with shops and an open market behind on the left. The covered market was destroyed by fire in 1983, then the property was resold to the council for development. Note the King's Head and shops in King Street.

Children in Acton Infant School, Oldham Terrace, in 1914 (see p. 13).

The Baptist church in Church Road during the ministry of the Revd E.S. Tongue (1913–19).

Priory Schools, Acton Lane, *c.* 1900. The Board schools were opened in 1883 and extended in 1895. They included a large central hall for public use.

Section Five

CHURCHFIELD ROAD

One of Richard's Cottages, at the west end of Churchfield Road, in 1960. The cottages, which were built c. *1870, were renowned for their beautiful gardens.*

Looking down Market Place in 1905. On the right is the William IV, to the left Churchfield Road.

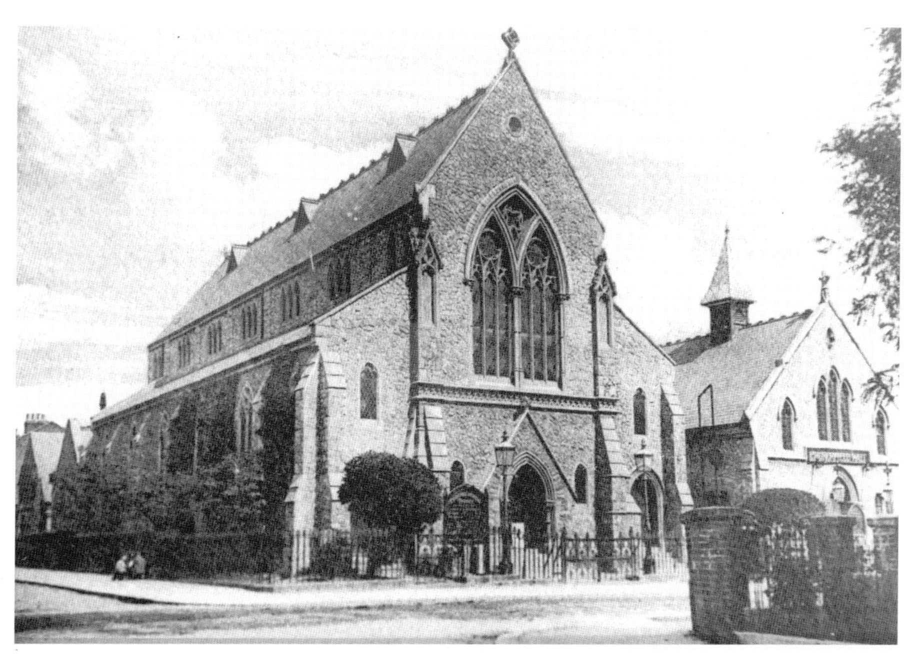

The Congregational church, schools and hall, *c.* 1900. The church was built by W. Tarring & Son and pulled down in 1976 to build flats.

The Tool Mart, 194 Churchfield Road, *c.* 1920. Founded by Arthur Mills, it later became Mills Bros, the famous tool suppliers. In 1990 the firm moved to Park Royal.

Churchfield Road looking west from the railway, *c.* 1895. On the left is the Station Hotel, in the distance Mr Blackwell's bus from Ealing to the station, and on the right is the high-class Baker's Stores and post office.

Acton Central station in 1976. Built in 1876, it replaced the first station of 1853. It is on the North London line.

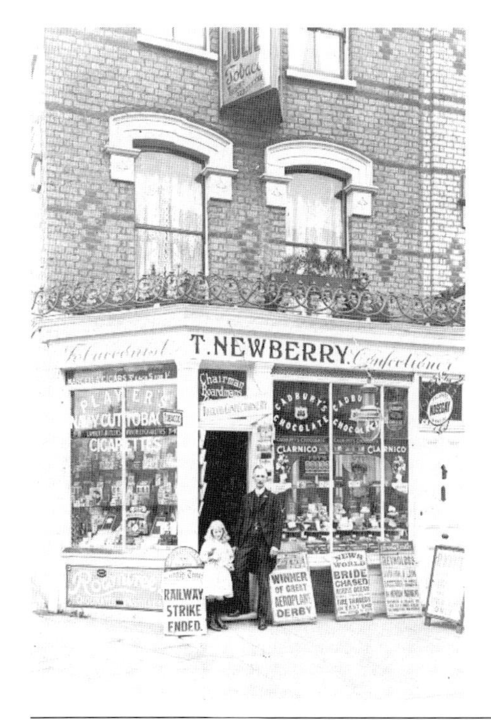

Mr Newberry and his daughter, *c.* 1911, outside the shop they have just acquired at 1 Churchfield Road.

Signal box and locomotive at Acton Central station in 1968. As the line crossed the Thames it became a link for other companies.

A North London train drawing into the station, *c.* 1900.

St John's Ambulance Brigade at Whitsun Carnival, 1959. They are by Acton Park at the corner of Churchfield Road East.

The obelisk in the Park, *c.* 1904. The Goldsmiths' Almshouses are visible behind (see also p. 110).

Section Six

EAST ACTON AND FRIAR'S PLACE

The doorway of East Acton manor house. This large house of c. *1680 was demolished in 1911. East Acton was for centuries a separate hamlet.*

Traction engine at East Acton in 1858. It was owned by Francis Hamilton of Friar's Place farm (see p. 64). The old Goldsmith's Arms (1821) is in the background.

East Acton village green. The houses on the left were built by J.W. & W.G. Ferris in 1929; on the right is the Chestnuts, sometime home of T. Wall (see p. 62).

St Dunstan's Church, *c.* 1906. Church and vicarage were built by the Goldsmiths' Company for the tenants on their estate. The church was consecrated in 1879.

St Dunstan's Vicarage, Friar's Place Lane. In 1940 it was leased by Acton Council as a wartime nursery; it has now been replaced by flats.

Entertainment at East Acton School in about May 1968. The school was opened in 1870 and rebuilt in 1925.

St Dunstan's Scout Troup, *c.* 1924. The Assistant Scout Master was S.M. Fullerton.

Friar's Place Lane in 1914. On left is Pembruge Villas and St Dunstan's Villas, built in 1872 and 1885 respectively.

A train on the North London line. This was the view north from the bridge of Friar's Place Lane towards the bridge of the abandoned Latimer Road and Acton Railway (removed 1916), and Friar's Place signal box.

'Stop-Me-and-Buy-One' in Friary Road. The railings of the GWR line are visible behind. Walls made sausages in the winter and ice-cream in the summer at their Friar's Place factory.

The Western Avenue Hotel, *c.* 1931. It became popular for club dinners. The first section of the Western Avenue was constructed in the 1920s and opened in 1928.

Section Seven

BEYOND THE GREAT WESTERN RAILWAY

The Great Western Main Line station in 1960. These buildings, erected in 1901, were demolished in 1969. The railway line was laid in 1837 and was Acton's first railway; the station was opened there in 1868.

No. 1 Leamington Park and Horn Lane, *c.* 1905. The house was lived in briefly by Dr W.G. Grace the cricketer in 1876, while doing his medical training at St Bartholomew's Hospital.

'A Farm Five Miles from Hyde Park!' (caption in the *Evening News*, 7 June 1927). This was Friar's Place Farm, also known as Narroway's or Snell's Farm (see p. 65). In the foreground is the last surviving piece of the medieval farm moat.

The Narroway family outside the farmhouse, *c.* 1895. From right to left: Elizabeth (wife), Hilda, Spencer, Joseph (farmer), farm manager, gardener, two maids.

The Home of Rest for Horses in 1900. The charity hired premises from Mr Narroway from 1890 to 1908.

Aerial view of part of the Great Western Railway Garden Village Estate in 1928. The 'Victory' bungalows of 1919 in Lowfield and Westfields roads can be seen, as well as part of North Acton playing fields with the remains of the other medieval moat.

Norman Way on the GWR Estate in 1930. These were some of the first houses to be built for GWR railwaymen working at Old Oak and Paddington.

St Gabriel's Church, Noel Road, *c.* 1969. The church was consecrated in 1931 but never completed.

Miss Noble's class at West Acton School in 1937. The children wear overalls, a different colour for each class, and are using the Montessori apparatus that was popular in Acton at the time.

Coronation celebrations at the school, May 1937. Children are dressed to represent countries of the Empire.

Gipsy Corner in 1905. Tomes, the monumental masons, is in the centre and the 'New' Acton Cemetery, established by the local board in 1894, is behind.

The cemetery chapels, *c.* 1905. They were designed by D.J. Ebbetts, Acton's surveyor.

Park Royal in 1903. The Royal Agricultural Society attempted to set up a permanent exhibition site in North Acton. Here it is being built.

T. Poore & Son helped in the construction and had a stall here from 1904 to 1906, when the site closed.

Varley Pumps, Standard Road, in 1952. After the First World War, Park Royal developed as a factory area. Varley Pumps was there from 1931 and later moved to Brentford.

The annexe and original factory of Landis & Gyr, 1970. They were in Victoria Road by 1927 and made metering equipment. The buildings were demolished in the 1970s.

A poster for Strachan's the coachbuilders, of Wales Farm Road, 1922.

Old-style milk-float of Wales Farm Dairy, *c.* 1910. J Franks owned the dairy and had premises in Horn Lane (see p. 43) and in East Acton, where he kept his cows, until 1927.

Acton Wells assembly room, as shown in a print probably used in advertisements before 1770. Minerals found in three wells near Old Oak produced a miniature spa from 1670 to 1775. Its bottled water was sold in London.

The Grand Junction Canal through Acton, 1980. It was made in 1801 and used to carry hay from Acton farms into London.

Acton Wells School being demolished in 1980. The school was opened in 1909.

May Day at Acton Wells School in the 1930s.

Boys in the Acton Wells School hall, 1937. The hall is decorated to commemorate the coronation of George VI. This large school in the north of Acton was opened in 1909 in anticipation of a neighbouring housing estate, but because of the First World War the area was taken over by munitions factories. Only after the war was it developed as a factory estate.

The Olympic Marathon of 1908, run from Windsor to the White City, passing the Railway Cottages in North Acton. These cottages at Willesden Junction (Acton) were built for employees by the London & North Western Railway Co. between 1876 and 1894.

Section Eight

DOWN SOUTH

Small labourers' cottages built soon after the enclosure of Turnham field in 1859.

Leaving work from Wilkinson Sword, *c.* 1917. The company established their sword and razor blade factory in Southfield Road in 1900 (see also p. 115).

Unloading millstones for Wilkinson Sword in 1917. They had a siding on the Hammersmith branch of the North & South Western Junction Railway which ran past the factory.

An aerial view of Wilkinson Sword, *c.* 1917.

St Peter's Temporary Church, Southfield Road, in 1907. The growth of housing in the area led to the need for a church.

St Peter's Church in 1974. It was based on St Paul's Outside the Walls, Rome, and consecrated in 1915.

St Peter's Day, *c.* 1920. The procession round the parish is passing Southfield Road recreation ground, which opened in 1908.

Posing for the camera at Southfield Infant School in 1911. Miss Dowling, headmistress from 1908 until her death in 1919, regularly put on shows for parents and friends.

All Saints' Church, Bollo Bridge Road, *c.* 1905. Built in 1872, it was the first church to the south of Acton. In the foreground is South Acton Recreation Ground, bought by the local board in 1889.

Demolition in the Bollo Bridge Road area, 1967–8. Tower blocks replaced many of the houses. All Saints tower can be seen on the left.

All Saints Boys' Brigade, *c.* 1906. They are photographed in the garden of the vicarage, Brouncker Road, with the vicar, the Revd Paton Hindley.

All Saints football team, 1917–18. Most churches, factories and schools had their sports teams in the inter-war period.

Townend's engineering works, Bollo Lane, from a catalogue cover of about 1902. Townend's manufactured laundry equipment from 1890 to 1939. The Bollo Brook ran through the yard.

Opposite: the Mayfair Laundry in 1960, which grew from the house laundry in front (1871) by constant addition. The laundry is now in a modern building in Stirling Road.

Right: taking in washing at home!

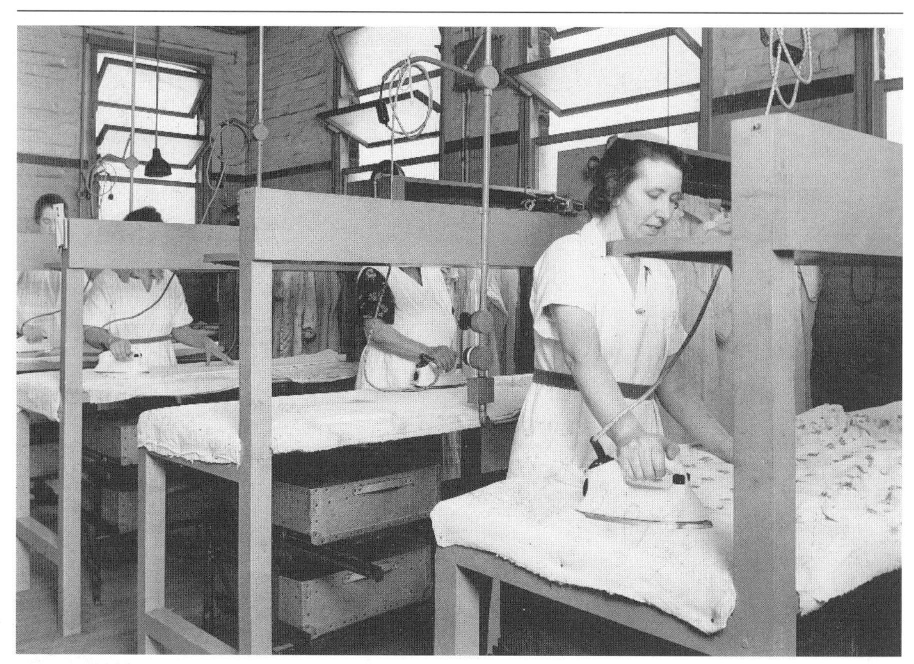

Ironing in the Mayfair Laundry in the 1920s.

The Laundry Proprietors' Club Committee outside the club in Strafford Road, 1898. Top row, from the left: G. Pratt, E.J.C. Gee, G.O. Gray, A. Perry, unknown, T.E. Davey; front row: J. Currell, W. Josling, W. Downes, A. Prevost.

Young Baptists carol singing in Park Road East, *c.* 1958. Their leader, Michael Loydell, is right of the lamp-post, holding the lantern.

Bollo Lane level crossing of the North London Railway, *c.* 1905.

Children of Rothschild School on a climbing frame, 1932. The school was opened in 1912 and closed in 1980.

Cleveland works and employees of Hewett the builder, *c.* 1913. The firm was responsible for building flats, houses and shops in Acton and Ealing before, during and after the Second World War. Alderman R.J. Hewett was mayor in 1925–6.

Beaumont Park Board Schools, Acton Lane, *c.* 1900. They were designed by Edward Monson, architect to the Board, with beautiful terracotta decoration, and built of local bricks by Hooper's of Avenue Road. Opened in 1891 as Acton's first free school, they replaced Acton Green School (see p. 90). From 1946 to 1961 they housed Priory Girls' Secondary School, then for a few years Cardinal Newman Roman Catholic School, until re-opening in 1976 as Acton Green School. This school closed in 1991, and the site was developed for housing.

Acton Green and Chiswick Park station, *c.* 1905. Opened on the new District Railway in 1879, it was renamed Chiswick Park in 1910 and rebuilt in 1932.

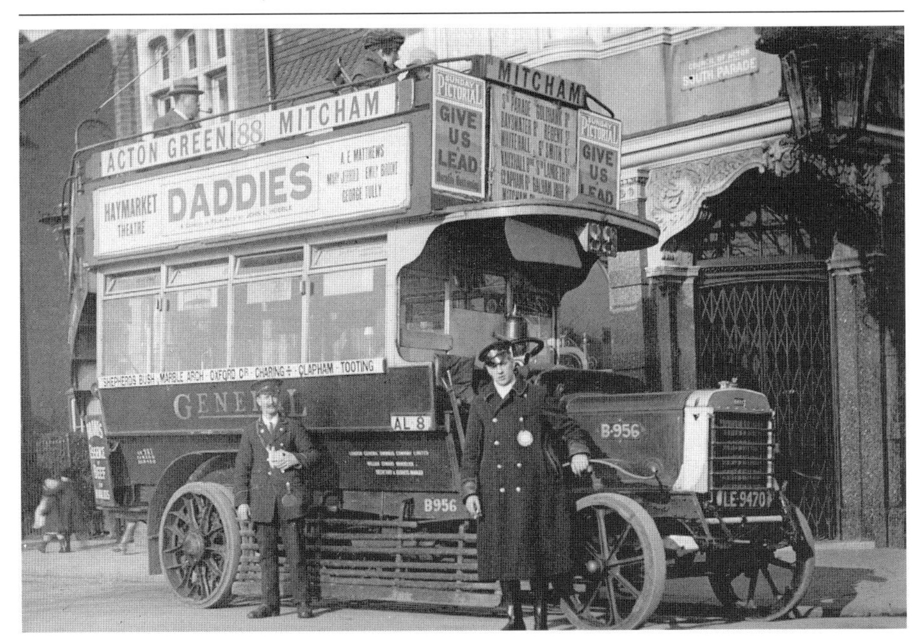

A 'B Type' General omnibus outside the Duke of Sussex, Acton Green, *c*. 1914.

St Alban's Church, Acton Green, in 1906. Designed by Edward Monson, it opened in 1888 and was demolished in 1970. To the right is Acton Green School (1870 to 1891).

Tennis courts, Fairlawn Park, Acton Green, before 1908. The estate was built in 1888 around a park. In 1934 the park itself was built over.

Bedford House, *c.* 1920. The early eighteenth-century building was half-covered by shops in 1924. It gave its name to the Bedford Park Estate, most of which was built in Acton.

Tower House, Bedford Park, *c.* 1905. It was built in 1878 by Jonathan Carr, to a design by Norman Shaw but using his own labour. Carr was the speculator responsible for building the central core of Bedford Park.

Section Nine

LOOKING WEST

A teddy bear made by J.K. Farnell & Co. of Acton Hill. The toy factory was based in Acton from 1905 to 1964 and made such famous bears as Winnie the Pooh.

Bishop Winnington-Ingram of London consecrating St Martin's Church, West Acton, in 1906. The architect was Edward Monson. Among the clergy are the new vicar, J.H. Blackman, lately curate of St Mary's and the rector of Acton, the Revd G. de Sausmarez.

The Uxbridge Road near the western border of Acton, *c.* 1905. On the right is King Edward Gardens (1902), on the left the small parks that replaced The Elms' ponds (see p. 11). The first electric trams began in 1901.

Wegg Avenue in 1893. Samuel Wegg of The Elms diverted Mill Lane to extend his villa in 1758. In 1901 the name was changed to Twyford Avenue.

Haberdashers' Aske's School for Girls, which was in Creffield Road from 1898 to 1974. Above: junior girls' gardening lesson, *c.* 1948. Below: upper IV cookery lesson at the school in 1949.

Creswick Road, Springfield Park Estate, *c.* 1905. This was the most prestigious estate in Acton, with large houses, wide roads and old trees.

Commemoration Day at Haberdashers' Aske's School, 1929. Miss D.M. Sprules, the headmistress, claimed 'the best exam results ever – a red-letter day for the school'.

Boys and masters at Acton County School in 1906, opened that year on a site in Woodlands. The masters are Thomson, Whittam, Clarke (headmaster) and Morgan.

Heathfield Lodge, Gunnersbury Lane, in 1965. An eighteenth-century house, it was enlarged in 1801 by John Soane, but has now been demolished. (see p. 12).

Section Ten

MAINLY MUNICIPAL

The arms of the Borough of Acton, incorporated 1921. The motto means 'May Acton flourish'. Note the oak tree with the arms of Middlesex above, the book for education and the wheel for industry.

The High Street in 1919. The offices of Acton Local Board, built 1871–2 on the site of the village pound, are on the left; on the right are buses of London General Omnibus Co. (For an earlier view, see p. 10.)

Acton Park in 1993 with café and Goldsmiths' Almshouses in the background. The park was acquired by the Local Board in 1888 to mark Queen Victoria's Jubilee.

Interior of Acton Baths, 1905. They were erected by the council and opened in 1904.

The public library in 1933. It was opened by the council in 1900 with a grant from Passmore Edwards, and designed by Maurice Adams.

Woodlands Park, *c.* 1909. Woodlands was acquired by the council in 1904 as part of its Crown Street development (see p. 48).

Leamington Park Hospital before demolition in 1984. It was bought by the council in 1905 and converted into an isolation hospital.

Acton town hall as it might have been in 1905. After the biggest controversy in Acton's history, much modified council offices were put up in Winchester Street in 1909; the town hall itself was not built until 1939.

The Grand Hall, 1933. This was the larger of the Acton swimming baths, which was covered over in the winter for functions. It was extended in 1926 with this imposing entrance from the High Street.

Mr F.A. Baldwin, Charter and first Mayor of Acton, with Mrs Baldwin in 1921. Mr Baldwin owned the Empire Laundry in the Steyne (see p. 43).

Neighbouring mayors arriving at the Globe cinema for the reading of the Charter of Incorporation, October 1921.

The High Street decorated for Incorporation Day, 1921.

The fire brigade outside the old fire station on Charter Day, 1921.

Mayor Harry Holmes beginning a Mayoral Avenue in Acton Park, 23 April 1931. The mayors here are, from left to right (with wives behind), Hamilton (1923), Mence (1929), Miss Smee (1924), Orange (1926), Hewett (1925), Middleton (1927), Street (1928) and Kent (1922). Seated are Mrs Baldwin (wife of the first mayor) with the Mayor and Mrs Holmes.

The Mayor and Mayoress, Cllr and Mrs Harry Holmes, processing along East Acton Lane to St Dunstan's Church for the Civic Service, November 1930.

Section Eleven

MAINLY VOLUNTARY – CARING FOR THE PEOPLE

Miss L.D. Ellis of the Society for Returning Women as Poor Law Guardians, in 1914. She was the first woman Guardian for Acton.

Seventeenth-century sheaves of carved wood. They were placed on the bread shelf in St Mary's Church on Sundays: after the service, 2 lb loaves were given to the poor (Lady Conway's bequest, 1680, and Crayle bequest, 1737). The practice ceased in 1890.

Jubilee Almshouses, the Steyne, 1965. Built in 1887 to replace earlier almshouses, they were demolished in 1972 (see p. 45).

Hospital Sunday, 1889. There was a procession and fund-raising effort annually to raise money for the Acton Dispensary and the West London Hospital. The Talbot public house is in the background.

The Goldsmith's Almshouses, Churchfield Road East, in 1950. They were built in 1811 from the charity of John Perryn, who left his East Acton estate to the Goldsmiths' Livery Company.

The Dolphin Coffee Tavern, Osborne Road, 1890. Set up to combat drunkenness in 1875, it sold cheap tea and coffee and provided a social venue.

The cottage hospital in 1915. Built in 1898 with the help of Passmore Edwards and maintained by voluntary contributions, it was extended in 1923 as the Acton War Memorial.

The medical staff outside the hospital in 1907.

A school clinic at the cottage hospital after 1908 when the new Education Act made such clinics compulsory.

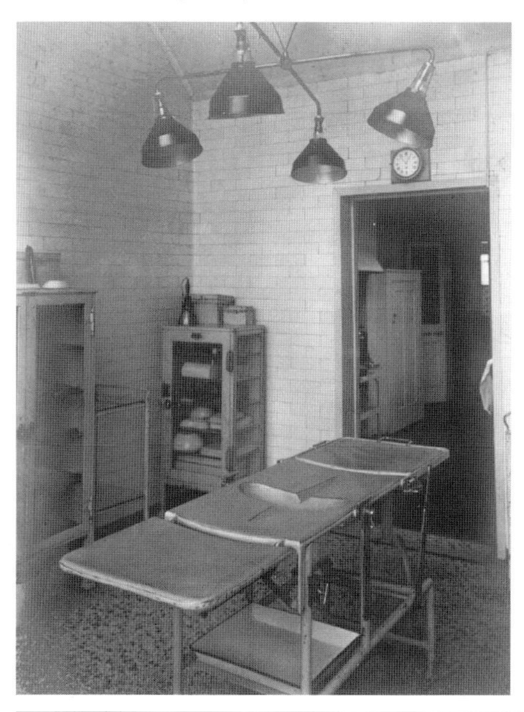

The early operating theatre at the hospital, *c.* 1910.

Acton Hill Brotherhood, a church organization for young men, giving supper to the unemployed in the old Wesleyan church, Gunnersbury Lane (see p. 14), perhaps in April 1911 when they were given a lecture on how to support their families on thirty shillings a week.

Toc H Ceremony of Light, 1960. This was the thirtieth anniversary guest night, held in the scouts' hall, Woodlands Park, of the Acton women's branch. The Mayor, Mrs Lilian Walker (seated, centre front), and Mayoress, Miss P. Cook (to her left), were present. There was a talk on the meaning of the lamps, the symbol of Toc H. The branch ran a club for the blind from about 1930 to 1994.

Section Twelve

WAR!

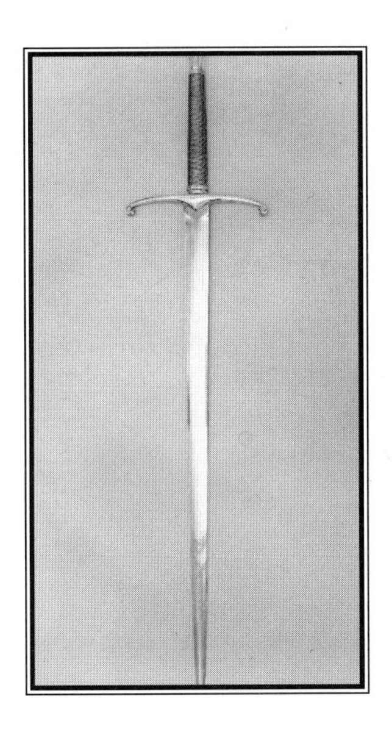

The Stalingrad Sword, made in 1943. It was forged by Wilkinson Sword of Acton by their swordsmith Tom Beasley. The inscription ran: TO THE STEEL-HEARTED CITIZENS OF STALINGRAD, THE GIFT OF KING GEORGE THE SIXTH, IN TOKEN OF THE HOMAGE OF THE BRITISH PEOPLE. It went on a tour of Britain before being presented to the Stalingrad representatives at the Teheran Conference of that year.

Munitions work at Park Royal in 1917. From 1914 the old exhibition site in Park Royal was used as a collection post for horses and also as a large munitions factory.

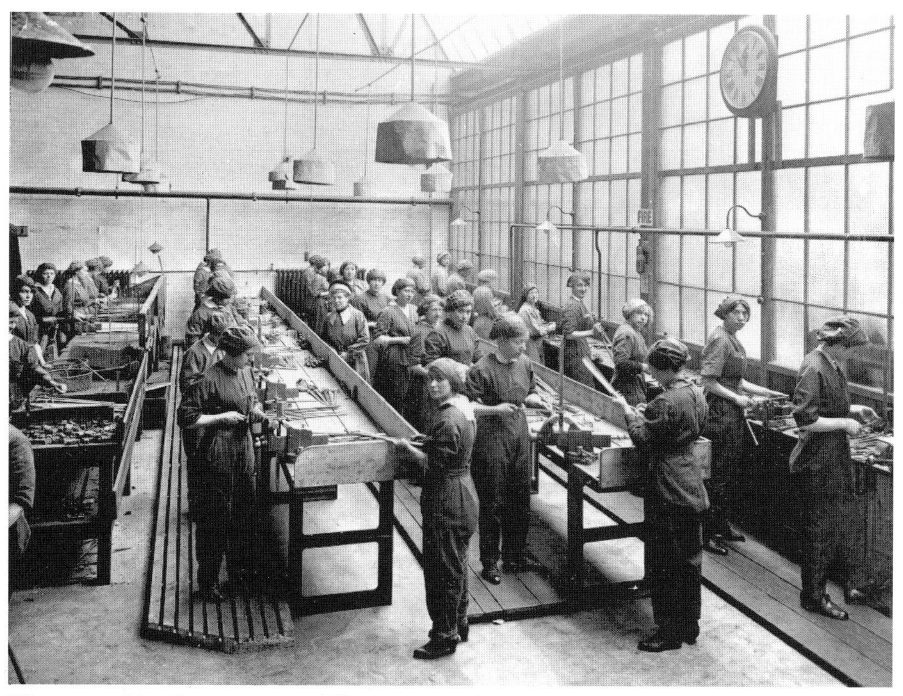

Women making bayonets at Wilkinson Sword, 1917. 2,250,000 bayonets were made there for use in the First World War.

Making aero engines at Napiers (see p. 33).

Edward John Gracie, DFC. Born in Acton in 1911, he served with distinction in the RAF from 1939, being made squadron-leader in 1943. He was shot down in February 1944.

Evacuation of 104 infants from West Acton School, 1939. The children were evacuated with their teachers to Holbeton in Devon.

Acton Civil Defence wardens, Post 7, July 1945. Left to right: (back) H.E. West, M. Mitchell, D.C. Evans, J.M. Barr, J.B. Lambert; (middle) E.M. Wilson, D/P/W F.J.C. Honey, E.A. Baker, M. Branson; (front) E.E. Bishop, D/P/W M.E. Endacott, P/W F. Bright, A/P/W E.P. Wilson, M. Burton.

Nos 18–20 The Link, GWR West Acton Estate, bombed 30 September 1940.

'Pre-fab' houses in Trinity Way, *c.* 1950. Priority was given to newly weds in this post-war housing scheme. Edith Stallwood stands outside her house – her husband, the Express milkman, is probably on his rounds!

The Mayor, Alderman J.A. Sparks MP, lays a wreath at the cenotaph outside St Mary's Church after the Armistice Day service in 1957. The mayoress and the Revd Richard Parsons, rector of Acton, are also present.

Section Thirteen

UNDER SAFEWAYS

The Odeon cinema (later the B & Q store) being demolished in 1990 to build the Safeway supermarket *(see also p. 123).*

Aerial view of the area where the supermarket was built in 1988. The Odeon is at the top on the right, St Mary's parish hall of 1933 is at the top in the middle. The open space was once Bank House (1630–1870). At the bottom Poore & Son trade from a block of houses dating from 1740 (see next page). The row of shops to the left includes Overall's (see p. 20).

Poore & Son, *c.* 1950. Established by Timothy Poore in King Street, it moved to the High Street in 1890, and was involved in much building work in Acton. It is now in Colville Road, South Acton.

King Street, *c.* 1940. The Odeon opened in 1937. Beyond it is the post office of 1911.

Nelson Place being demolished in 1971. It was built on the Bank House site after 1870. At the back is the rear entrance to Poore & Son and C.W.C. Poore's car.

Part of Steyne Road in 1971, just round the corner from Nelson Place, with Skinner's the electrical shop on the corner. This property was also built *c.* 1870.

St Mary's Rectory, 1990. It was built in 1925 and succeeded earlier rectories, the second lasting from 1725 to 1925.

Rectory Cottage in 1892. This was originally Madame Garway's Cottage of 1616, and was added to from time to time, acting as a school from 1812 to 1840. It was later a youth club but was demolished in 1924 to make a front garden for the new rectory.

Further Reading

There are several antiquarian and out-of-date books about Acton. For up-to-date information see *The Victoria County History of Middlesex*, Vol. VII (London, 1892), and B. Cherry and N. Pevsner, *Buildings of England: London 3, Northwest* (London, 1991). There are also the 'Acton Past and Present' series of booklets (1984–95) which cover many aspects of Acton's life and history. All these may be seen at the Ealing Local History Library, which also has copies of the index to the *Acton Gazette* 1900–37, produced by members of the Acton History Group. This is an ongoing work. The *Acton Historian* is published twice yearly by the Acton History Group, 42 Avenue Gardens, London W3 8HB.

Acknowledgements

The authors thank the many members and friends of the Acton History Group who have lent photographs for inclusion in this book:

the Rector of Acton • Acton Baptist Church • Acton High School
Acton Hill Church • Acton Hospital • Bird's Eye Walls • David Bowater
the British Library (p. 64 bottom and p. 106 top) • Philip Burton
Mrs O. Caesar • Mr G.W. Coe • *Country Life* • Tony Cozens
Ted Crouchman • Ealing Tertiary College • Harry Edwards • P.W. Elkins
H. Engleheart • Mrs V. Faithfull • Mr and Mrs R.N. Franks • John Goodwin
the Greater London Record Office • Mrs Amy Green • Mr and Mrs C. Green
Fullers Griffin Brewery • Guildhall Library, Print Dept
Gunnersbury Park Museum • Haberdashers' Aske's School for Girls
Mrs E. Harrington • the Johnson Group • Miss Marina Jones
the John Lewis Partnership Archive • Lucas Electrical Systems • Tony Mawby
the Mayfair Laundry • Mills Bros • Malcolm Mitchell
Napier Power Heritage • Keith Noble • Messrs Overalls • John Poore
Mrs Margaret Rowland • St Martin's Church • C.S. Smeaton
Southfield School • Mrs M. Stuckey • Miss M.W. Thorley • George Twyman
Philip Warren • West Acton School • Wilkinson Sword
the Revd J.M.V. Willmington.

Royalties from this book are to be given to the Acton History Fund which aids preservation and conservation projects and the recording of Acton history.

BRITAIN IN OLD PHOTOGRAPHS

To order any of these titles please telephone Littlehampton Book Services on 01903 721596

ALDERNEY

Alderney: A Second Selection, *B Bonnard*

BEDFORDSHIRE

Bedfordshire at Work, *N Lutt*

BERKSHIRE

Maidenhead, *M Hayles & D Hedges*
Around Maidenhead, *M Hayles & B Hedges*
Reading, *P Southerton*
Reading: A Second Selection, *P Southerton*
Sandhurst and Crowthorne, *K Dancy*
Around Slough, *J Hunter & K Hunter*
Around Thatcham, *P Allen*
Around Windsor, *B Hedges*

BUCKINGHAMSHIRE

Buckingham and District, *R Cook*
High Wycombe, *R Goodearl*
Around Stony Stratford, *A Lambert*

CHESHIRE

Cheshire Railways, *M Hitches*
Chester, *S Nichols*

CLWYD

Clwyd Railways, *M Hitches*

CLYDESDALE

Clydesdale, *Lesmahagow Parish Historical Association*

CORNWALL

Cornish Coast, *T Bowden*
Falmouth, *P Gilson*
Lower Fal, *P Gilson*
Around Padstow, *M McCarthy*
Around Penzance, *J Holmes*
Penzance and Newlyn, *J Holmes*
Around Truro, *A Lyne*
Upper Fal, *P Gilson*

CUMBERLAND

Cockermouth and District, *J Bernard Bradbury*
Keswick and the Central Lakes, *J Marsh*
Around Penrith, *F Boyd*
Around Whitehaven, *H Fancy*

DERBYSHIRE

Derby, *D Buxton*
Around Matlock, *D Barton*

DEVON

Colyton and Seaton, *T Gosling*
Dawlish and Teignmouth, *G Gosling*
Devon Aerodromes, *K Saunders*
Exeter, *P Thomas*
Exmouth and Budleigh Salterton, *T Gosling*
From Haldon to Mid-Dartmoor, *T Hall*
Honiton and the Otter Valley, *J Yallop*
Around Kingsbridge, *K Tanner*
Around Seaton and Sidmouth, *T Gosling*
Seaton, Axminster and Lyme Regis, *T Gosling*

DORSET

Around Blandford Forum, *B Cox*
Bournemouth, *M Colman*
Bridport and the Bride Valley, *J Burrell & S Humphries*
Dorchester, *T Gosling*
Around Gillingham, *P Crocker*

DURHAM

Darlington, *G Flynn*
Darlington: A Second Selection, *G Flynn*
Durham People, *M Richardson*
Houghton-le-Spring and Hetton-le-Hole, *K Richardson*
Houghton-le-Spring and Hetton-le-Hole: A Second Selection, *K Richardson*
Sunderland, *S Miller & B Bell*
Teesdale, *D Coggins*
Teesdale: A Second Selection, *P Raine*
Weardale, *J Crosby*
Weardale: A Second Selection, *J Crosby*

DYFED

Aberystwyth and North Ceredigion, *Dyfed Cultural Services Dept*
Haverfordwest, *Dyfed Cultural Services Dept*
Upper Tywi Valley, *Dyfed Cultural Services Dept*

ESSEX

Around Grays, *B Evans*

GLOUCESTERSHIRE

Along the Avon from Stratford to Tewkesbury, *J Jeremiah*
Cheltenham: A Second Selection, *R Whiting*
Cheltenham at War, *P Gill*
Cirencester, *J Welsford*
Around Cirencester, *E Cuss & P Griffiths*
Forest, The, *D Mullin*
Gloucester, *J Voyce*
Around Gloucester, *A Sutton*
Gloucester: From the Walwin Collection, *J Voyce*
North Cotswolds, *D Viner*
Severn Vale, *A Sutton*
Stonehouse to Painswick, *A Sutton*
Stroud and the Five Valleys, *S Gardiner & L Padin*
Stroud and the Five Valleys: A Second Selection, *S Gardiner & L Padin*
Stroud's Golden Valley, *S Gardiner & L Padin*
Stroudwater and Thames & Severn Canals, *E Cuss & S Gardiner*
Stroudwater and Thames & Severn Canals: A Second Selection, *E Cuss & S Gardiner*
Tewkesbury and the Vale of Gloucester, *C Hilton*
Thornbury to Berkeley, *J Hudson*
Uley, Dursley and Cam, *A Sutton*
Wotton-under-Edge to Chipping Sodbury, *A Sutton*

GWYNEDD

Anglesey, *M Hitches*
Gwynedd Railways, *M Hitches*
Around Llandudno, *M Hitches*
Vale of Conwy, *M Hitches*

HAMPSHIRE

Gosport, *J Sadden*
Portsmouth, *P Rogers & D Francis*

HEREFORDSHIRE

Herefordshire, *A Sandford*

HERTFORDSHIRE

Barnet, *I Norrie*
Hitchin, *A Fleck*
St Albans, *S Mullins*
Stevenage, *M Appleton*

ISLE OF MAN

The Tourist Trophy, *B Snelling*

ISLE OF WIGHT

Newport, *D Parr*
Around Ryde, *D Parr*

JERSEY

Jersey: A Third Selection, *R Lemprière*

KENT

Bexley, *M Scott*
Broadstairs and St Peter's, *J Whyman*
Bromley, Keston and Hayes, *M Scott*
Canterbury: A Second Selection, *D Butler*
Chatham and Gillingham, *P MacDougall*
Chatham Dockyard, *P MacDougall*
Deal, *J Broady*
Early Broadstairs and St Peter's, *B Wootton*
East Kent at War, *D Collyer*
Eltham, *J Kennett*
Folkestone: A Second Selection, *A Taylor & E Rooney*
Goudhurst to Tenterden, *A Guilmant*
Gravesend, *R Hiscock*
Around Gravesham, *R Hiscock & D Grierson*
Herne Bay, *J Hawkins*
Lympne Airport, *D Collyer*
Maidstone, *I Hales*
Margate, *R Clements*
RAF Hawkinge, *R Humphreys*
RAF Manston, *RAF Manston History Club*
RAF Manston: A Second Selection, *RAF Manston History Club*
Ramsgate and Thanet Life, *D Perkins*
Romney Marsh, *E Carpenter*
Sandwich, *C Wanostrocht*
Around Tonbridge, *C Bell*
Tunbridge Wells, *M Rowlands & I Beavis*
Tunbridge Wells: A Second Selection, *M Rowlands & I Beavis*
Around Whitstable, *C Court*
Wingham, Adisham and Littlebourne, *M Crane*

LANCASHIRE

Around Barrow-in-Furness, *J Garbutt & J Marsh*
Blackpool, *C Rothwell*
Bury, *J Hudson*
Chorley and District, *J Smith*
Fleetwood, *C Rothwell*
Heywood, *J Hudson*
Around Kirkham, *C Rothwell*
Lancashire North of the Sands, *J Garbutt & J Marsh*
Around Lancaster, *S Ashworth*
Lytham St Anne's, *C Rothwell*
North Fylde, *C Rothwell*
Radcliffe, *J Hudson*
Rossendale, *B Moore & N Dunnachie*

LEICESTERSHIRE

Around Ashby-de-la-Zouch, *K Hillier*
Charnwood Forest, *I Keil, W Humphrey & D Wix*
Leicester, *D Burton*
Leicester: A Second Selection, *D Burton*
Melton Mowbray, *T Hickman*
Around Melton Mowbray, *T Hickman*
River Soar, *D Wix, P Shacklock & I Keil*
Rutland, *T Clough*
Vale of Belvoir, *T Hickman*
Around the Welland Valley, *S Mastoris*

LINCOLNSHIRE

Grimsby, *J Tierney*
Around Grimsby, *J Tierney*
Grimsby Docks, *J Tierney*
Lincoln, *D Cuppleditch*

Scunthorpe, *D Taylor*
Skegness, *W Kime*
Around Skegness, *W Kime*

LONDON

Balham and Tooting, *P Loobey*
Crystal Palace, Penge & Anerley, *M Scott*
Greenwich and Woolwich, *K Clark*
Hackney: A Second Selection, *D Mander*
Lewisham and Deptford, *J Coulter*
Lewisham and Deptford: A Second Selection, *J Coulter*
Streatham, *P Loobey*
Around Whetstone and North Finchley, *J Heathfield*
Woolwich, *B Evans*

MONMOUTHSHIRE

Chepstow and the River Wye, *A Rainsbury*
Monmouth and the River Wye, *Monmouth Museum*

NORFOLK

Great Yarmouth, *M Teun*
Norwich, *M Colman*
Wymondham and Attleborough, *P Yaxley*

NORTHAMPTONSHIRE

Around Stony Stratford, *A Lambert*

NOTTINGHAMSHIRE

Arnold and Bestwood, *M Spick*
Arnold and Bestwood: A Second Selection, *M Spick*
Changing Face of Nottingham, *G Oldfield*
Mansfield, *Old Mansfield Society*
Around Newark, *T Warner*
Nottingham: 1944–1974, *D Whitworth*
Sherwood Forest, *D Ottewell*
Victorian Nottingham, *M Payne*

OXFORDSHIRE

Around Abingdon, *P Horn*
Banburyshire, *M Barnett & S Gosling*
Burford, *A Jewell*
Around Didcot and the Hagbournes, *B Lingham*
Garsington, *M Gunther*
Around Henley-on-Thames, *S Ellis*
Oxford: The University, *J Rhodes*
Thame to Watlington, *N Hood*
Around Wallingford, *D Beasley*
Witney, *T Worley*
Around Witney, *C Mitchell*
Witney District, *T Worley*
Around Woodstock, *J Bond*

POWYS

Brecon, *Brecknock Museum*
Welshpool, *E Bredsdorff*

SHROPSHIRE

Shrewsbury, *D Trumper*
Whitchurch to Market Drayton, *M Morris*

SOMERSET

Bath, *J Hudson*
Bridgwater and the River Parrett, *R Fitzhugh*
Bristol, *D Moorcroft & N Campbell-Sharp*
Changing Face of Keynsham,
B Lowe & M Whitehead
Chard and Ilminster, *G Gosling & F Huddy*
Crewkerne and the Ham Stone Villages,
G Gosling & F Huddy
Around Keynsham and Saltford, *B Lowe & T Brown*
Midsomer Norton and Radstock, *C Howell*
Somerton, Ilchester and Langport, *G Gosling & F Huddy*
Taunton, *N Chipchase*
Around Taunton, *N Chipchase*
Wells, *C Howell*
Weston-Super-Mare, *S Poole*
Around Weston-Super-Mare, *S Poole*
West Somerset Villages, *K Houghton & L Thomas*

STAFFORDSHIRE

Aldridge, *J Farrow*
Bilston, *E Rees*
Black Country Transport: Aviation, *A Brew*
Around Burton upon Trent, *G Sowerby & R Farman*
Bushbury, *A Chatwin, M Mills & E Rees*
Around Cannock, *M Mills & S Belcher*
Around Leek, *R Poole*
Lichfield, *H Clayton & K Simmons*
Around Pattingham and Wombourne, *M Griffiths, P Leigh & M Mills*
Around Rugeley, *T Randall & J Anslow*
Smethwick, *J Maddison*
Stafford, *J Anslow & T Randall*
Around Stafford, *J Anslow & T Randall*
Stoke-on-Trent, *I Lawley*
Around Tamworth, *R Sulima*
Around Tettenhall and Codsall, *M Mills*
Tipton, Wednesbury and Darlaston, *R Pearson*
Walsall, *D Gilbert & M Lewis*
Wednesbury, *I Bott*
West Bromwich, *R Pearson*

SUFFOLK

Ipswich: A Second Selection, *D Kindred*
Around Ipswich, *D Kindred*
Around Mildenhall, *C Dring*
Southwold to Aldeburgh, *H Phelps*
Around Woodbridge, *H Phelps*

SURREY

Cheam and Belmont, *P Berry*
Croydon, *S Bligh*
Dorking and District, *K Harding*
Around Dorking, *A Jackson*
Around Epsom, *P Berry*
Farnham: A Second Selection, *J Parratt*
Around Haslemere and Hindhead, *T Winter & G Collyer*
Richmond, *Richmond Local History Society*
Sutton, *P Berry*

SUSSEX

Arundel and the Arun Valley, *J Godfrey*
Bishopstone and Seaford, *P Pople & P Berry*
Brighton and Hove, *J Middleton*
Brighton and Hove: A Second Selection, *J Middleton*
Around Crawley, *M Goldsmith*
Hastings, *P Haines*
Hastings: A Second Selection, *P Haines*
Around Haywards Heath, *J Middleton*
Around Heathfield, *A Gillet & B Russell*
Around Heathfield: A Second Selection,
A Gillet & B Russell
High Weald, *B Harwood*
High Weald: A Second Selection, *B Harwood*
Horsham and District, *T Wales*
Lewes, *J Middleton*
RAF Tangmere, *A Saunders*
Around Rye, *A Dickinson*
Around Worthing, *S White*

WARWICKSHIRE

Along the Avon from Stratford to Tewkesbury, *J Jeremiah*
Bedworth, *J Burton*
Coventry, *D McGrory*
Around Coventry, *D McGrory*
Nuneaton, *S Clews & S Vaughan*
Around Royal Leamington Spa, *J Cameron*
Around Royal Leamington Spa: A Second Selection,
J Cameron
Around Warwick, *R Booth*

WESTMORLAND

Eden Valley, *J Marsh*
Kendal, *M & P Duff*
South Westmorland Villages, *J Marsh*
Westmorland Lakes, *J Marsh*

WILTSHIRE

Around Amesbury, *P Daniels*
Chippenham and Lacock, *A Wilson & M Wilson*
Around Corsham and Box, *A Wilson & M Wilson*
Around Devizes, *D Buxton*
Around Highworth, *G Tanner*
Around Highworth and Faringdon, *G Tanner*
Around Malmesbury, *A Wilson*
Marlborough: A Second Selection, *P Colman*
Around Melksham,
Melksham and District Historical Association
Nadder Valley, *R. Sawyer*
Salisbury, *P Saunders*
Salisbury: A Second Selection, *P Daniels*
Salisbury: A Third Selection, *P Daniels*
Around Salisbury, *P Daniels*
Swindon: A Third Selection, *The Swindon Society*
Swindon: A Fourth Selection, *The Swindon Society*
Trowbridge, *M Marshman*
Around Wilton, *P Daniels*
Around Wootton Bassett, Cricklade and Purton, *T Sharp*

WORCESTERSHIRE

Evesham to Bredon, *F Archer*
Around Malvern, *K Smith*
Around Pershore, *M Dowty*
Redditch and the Needle District, *R Saunders*
Redditch: A Second Selection, *R Saunders*
Around Tenbury Wells, *D Green*
Worcester, *M Dowty*
Around Worcester, *R Jones*
Worcester in a Day, *M Dowty*
Worcestershire at Work, *R Jones*

YORKSHIRE

Huddersfield: A Second Selection, *H Wheeler*
Huddersfield: A Third Selection, *H Wheeler*
Leeds Road and Rail, *R Vickers*
Pontefract, *R van Riel*
Scarborough, *D Coggins*
Scarborough's War Years, *R Percy*
Skipton and the Dales, *Friends of the Craven Museum*
Around Skipton-in-Craven, *Friends of the Craven Museum*
Yorkshire Wolds, *I & M Sumner*